Contents

Welcome — 2

1 Let's stay healthy — 4

2 Let's be green — 12

Review Units 1 and 2 — 20

3 Natural world — 22

4 All about water — 30

Review Units 3 and 4 — 38

5 Fair future — 40

6 Sharing the message — 48

Review Units 5 and 6 — 56

Goodbye — 58

Celebrations — 60

Word connections — 62

 **to our summer camp!**

1 **Look and write.**

| city x 2   ~~town~~   village   summer camp   camp leader |
| Turkey   Argentina   Spain   China |

1

Hi, I'm Mateo.
I live in a _town_
in _____ .

2

Hello, my name is Julia. I
come from a _____
in _____ .

3

Hello! I'm Su. I come from a
_____ in _____ .

4

Hi, my name's Omer and I live in a
_____ in _____ .

5

Hi! I'm Anita. I'm the _____
here at the Rise and Shine _____ .
Have a great summer, everyone!

2 (0.06) **Read and write. Then listen and check.**

Anita: Welcome to the camp! What [1] _are you going to do_ (you / do) this summer?

Su: We [2] _____ (have) a lot of fun!

Mateo: I [3] _____ (play) on the rope swing.

Julia: I [4] _____ (walk) in the forest!

Anita: Where [5] _____ (you / sleep)?

Omer: We [6] _____ (sleep) in that cabin!

Su: We [7] _____ (not / eat) in the kitchen!

We [8] _____ (have) our meals at
that picnic table. It's going to be a great summer!

2

Extra time? Say in alphabetical order: roof   cabin   gate   door   seat   window

3 Read and write.

| Mateo   Omer   ~~Julia~~   Mateo and Su   All the children |

1 _Julia_ _____ is going to write a song.
2 _____ is going to perform on stage with Julia.
3 _____ are going to play in a band together.
4 _____ is going to write a film.
5 _____ are going to design the show programme.

4 💬 Read, find and write. Then, ask and answer.

1 We're going to put on a _show_ _____
   together!

2 I like music. I'm going to write a
   _____! What do you think?

3 I like getting up in front of a lot of people.
   I'm going to perform on _____!

4 I play the guitar and you play the drums.
   Maybe we could play in a _____
   together!

5 I like pretending to be someone else.
   I'm going to act in a _____!

6 I like drawing. I'm going to design a _____
   for the show! What do you reckon?

i	o	p	p	b	p	j	l	r
x	j	r	r	t	e	u	o	s
a	x	g	o	c	f	h	g	o
m	i	y	g	k	i	j	l	n
u	g	s	r	i	l	v	s	g
b	b	h	a	e	m	v	t	b
a	w	o	m	x	b	h	a	n
n	g	w	m	s	c	a	g	p
d	c	i	e	n	h	u	e	x

◁ _What are you going to do in the summer camp show?_

◁ _That sounds great!_   _I'm going to play in a band!_ ▷

I can shine! ✳

5 Write.

My friends and I are going to put on a 'Make the world
a better place' show! This is my programme.

In the show, I'm going to _____

_____

Staying healthy	Climate change	Fair future
Green homes	Saving water	Sharing the message

Extra time? MAKE THE WORLD A BETTER PLACE SHOW.
Use the letters and make a new word.

Let's stay healthy

Let's review!

Name four types of fruit or vegetable.

_____ _____

_____ _____

Lesson 1 ➡ Vocabulary

1 Look and write. What's the hidden food?

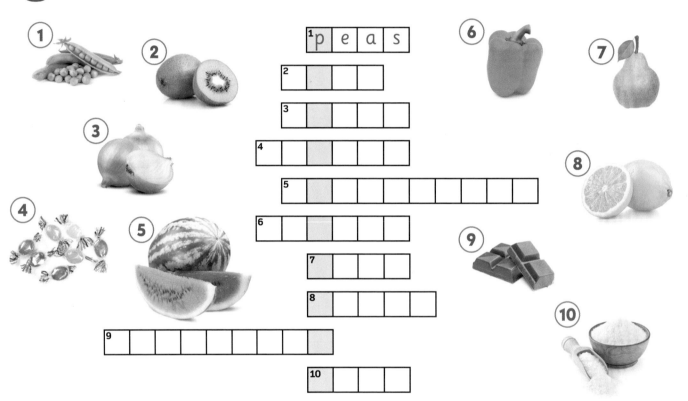

| 1 | p | e | a | s |

2 Look at Activity 1. Write.

1 Watermelons, _lemons_ , _____ and _____ are types of fruit.

2 Onions, _____ and _____ are types of vegetable.

3 Some people put _____ on food to add flavour but it isn't very healthy.

4 Sweets and _____ contain a lot of sugar.

Tell me!

Write the food words from your favourite to your least favourite.

My favourite food   My least favourite food

_____ _____ _____ _____ _____

4

Extra time? Which types of food are healthy? Which aren't healthy?

1 🎧 1.04 **Read and write. Then listen and answer.** *True* **or** *false?*

1 Sally ___found___ (find) some peppers.   T

2 She _____ (not / find) any onions. ___

3 She _____ (see) some lemons. ___

4 She _____ (not / see) any kiwis. ___

5 She _____ (put) the bag of pears in the fridge. ___

6 She _____ (eat) one of the pears on the way home. ___

2 **Look and write in the past form.**

> go cut find ~~make~~ put not see eat not make

Last Saturday I ¹___made___ (make) lunch for my family! I ²_____ to the market in the morning to get some fresh fruit and vegetables. I ³_____ some delicious red peppers, onions, a cucumber and a watermelon. But I ⁴_____ any peas or kiwis. I ⁵_____ a fruit salad or a vegetable salad. I made a fruit *and* vegetable salad! I ⁶_____ the vegetables and the watermelon into small squares. Then I ⁷_____ them in the bowl and added some lemon. Yum! We all ⁸_____ lunch in the garden together!

I can shine!

3 **Imagine you made lunch for your family last weekend. Write.**

Last weekend, I made a delicious lunch for my family. I...

_____
_____
_____

make
eat
find
put
see

Extra time? When you eat something, say the word in English to help you remember!

1 **Read and number.**

	a	The traveller offered to make his medicine soup.
1	**b**	The traveller met some villagers who were sick.
	c	The villagers found a lot of vegetables for the soup.
	d	The traveller showed the villagers his medicine stone.
	e	The traveller gave the villagers his stone and left.
	f	Everyone ate the soup together and the villagers felt better.

2 **Read and write.**

> cough   sick   ~~headache~~
> temperature   medicine   doctor

1 The woman has a ___headache.___

2 She also feels _____ .

3 The man has a _____ .

4 And he also has a _____ .

5 Now the villagers have the medicine stone,
they don't have to go to the _____ .

6 And they don't have to take _____ .

> **Let's imagine!**
>
> *Tell me about the story!*
>
> *'Medicine soup' is a*
> **folk tale / true story.**
>
> *The story setting is*
>
> _____ .
>
> *My favourite character is*
>
> _____ .

I can shine!

3 **Plan a healthy meal to help a sick friend feel better.**

1 What's the matter with your friend?

_____

2 What healthy meal are you going to make for him or her?

_____

Extra time? Why is it important to eat healthy food?

1 Read and circle.

Leo

Maria

Zac and Lisa

1 What was the matter with Leo?
He had a (cough) / **temperature**.

2 Did Leo have a headache?
No, he didn't. / **Yes, he did.**

3 Did Maria take some medicine?
Yes, she did. / **No she didn't.**

4 What did Zac and Lisa do?
They **went to the doctor** / **didn't go to the doctor**.

2 🎧 1.12 Read and write. Then listen and check.

Doctor: Hi, Amelie. What's the matter?

Amelie: I have a cough.

Doctor: Well, you should avoid drinking anything chilled.

Amelie: In other ¹____words,____ I shouldn't drink cold drinks.

Doctor: That's right. In fact, warm drinks might be beneficial.

Amelie: So, you ²_____ I should drink warm drinks.

Doctor: Yes. And take this medicine half an hour before meals.

Amelie: In other words, I should
³_____
thirty minutes before I eat.

Doctor: Yes! And you'll be as good as new in no time!

Amelie: So you mean that I should
⁴_____.

Doctor: Exactly!

Let's build!
Imagine your partner was sick last week. Ask and answer.

What was the matter?

Did you go to the doctor?

I can shine! ✦

3 Talk with a partner. Give advice. Then listen and repeat using different words.

You should get some professional advice.

So, you mean I should go to the doctor.

Pronunciation Colour the two sounds in red and blue.
b**e**d oth**er** mother well teacher flower leg yes

1 **Read and match. Then look and write.**

1 curry   **a** a dish from Japan made of small balls of cold rice with vegetables, eggs or raw fish

2 sushi   **b** a thick, liquid food made of milk

3 taco   **c** a dish made of meat, fish or vegetables cooked with hot spices

4 yoghurt   **d** a dish from Mexico made of a flour pancake shell filled with meat, fish or vegetables

_____ _____ _____ _____

2 1.16 **Listen and tick (✓) the food that Jack and Flora say. Then listen again and circle.**

International Café Menu

Tacos
meat ☐
fish ☐
vegetable ☐

Sushi
fish ☐
vegetable ☐

Curry
vegetable ☐
chicken ☐
fish ☐

1 Flora **likes / doesn't like** fish.

2 Jack **likes / doesn't like** fish.

3 Jack wants to eat vegetable **tacos / curry**.

4 Jack **likes / doesn't like** very spicy food.

5 Flora wants to eat **vegetable / chicken** curry.

6 Flora **likes / doesn't like** spicy food.

> *What food from another country do you want to try? Why?*

Extra time? What's your favourite healthy food from your country?

1 **Read and answer.**

Which adjectives does Luis use to describe food?

Luis_87*

Add a comment

Hi! I am from Mexico. The food in my country is healthy and delicious.

My favourite international food is pizza because I love cheese. Yesterday, I went to a pizza restaurant. I had a pizza with cheese and pineapple. It was wonderful! The fruit on the pizza was healthy, too.

I also like curry because I love spicy food. Fish curry is amazing and I like vegetable curry, too. I want to learn how to make curry.

2 Give it a go **Plan your online message about international food.**

Where are you from?	
What is the food like in your country?	
What is your favourite international food?	
When did you last eat it?	
What was it like?	
What other international food do you like? Why?	

I can shine!

3 **Write your online message about international food.**

Check your work! Read your online message again. Did you spell the new adjectives correctly?

1 **Look and write.**

Yesterday

1 o_____

Lucy

2 p_____

3 s_____

4 c_____

5 h_____

6 m_____

7 c_____

8 feel s_____

2 (1.19) **Look at Activity 1 and write. Then listen and check.**

1 Lucy's mum / have cough?

Did Lucy's mum have a cough?   _Yes, she did._

2 Lucy's dad / have temperature?

_____ ? _____ .

3 Lucy's brother / go to the doctor?

_____ ? _____ .

4 Lucy's sister / feel sick?

_____ ? _____ .

5 What / Lucy's dad / do?

_____ ? _____ .

6 What / Lucy / make?

_____ ? _____ .

3 **Lucy's dad went to the doctor. Repeat the doctor's advice using different words and expressions from the unit.**

You shouldn't go to the office for at least a week.   stay at home / seven days

You must take your medicine on an empty stomach.   take medicine / before breakfast

Extra time? I'm a fruit. I'm small and green. My skin is furry but I taste sweet! What am I?

1 Think and write. Then add an extra word to each category.

> kiwi lemon sushi pear tacos watermelon cakes onion salt
> pea peppers sweets curry chocolate yoghurt milkshake

Healthy food   **Unhealthy food**

We can eat a lot
of these foods.

We can
eat these foods
sometimes.

We shouldn't eat a
lot of these foods.

_____   _____   _____

_____   _____   _____

_____   _____   _____

2 Complete your journal.

Step 1: Imagine a lunch you made for your class last week. How did you make the meal?

Step 2: Write your journal in the past form. Describe the food and include food pictures.

Step 3: Finish, check and read your journal.

My healthy class lunch!

Starter: Pepper and onion salad

I found delicious, fresh vegetables in the school garden. It was wonderful!

Main course: Fish curry

I saw an interesting recipe for curry in my dad's recipe book. So I cut up the fish and vegetables and made an amazing curry. It wasn't very spicy!

Dessert: Yoghurt and honey

I made a healthy Greek dessert. Yum!

---

3 Think and write.

Unit 1

My favourite food: _____

A difficult word: _____

An interesting international food: _____

> **Tip!**
> You can say that
> you eat a meal or
> have a meal!

Home-school link Tell your family about your favourite healthy food.

2 Let's be green

Lesson 1 ➡ Vocabulary

1 Read and match.

1 large	d	**2** light	☐	**3** tidy	☐	**4** full	☐	**5** soft	☐

a messy   **b** dark   **c** hard   **d** tiny   **e** empty

2 Look at Activity 1. Then look and write.

1 What a ___large___ house!

2 What a _____ house!

3 Luca's bedroom is _____ !

4 Alex's bedroom is _____ !

5 This sofa is _____ !

6 This chair is _____ !

7 It's a _____ room in the mornings.

8 It's a _____ room.

9 Rita's wardrobe is _____ !

10 Rose's wardrobe is _____ !

Tell me!

Describe your bedroom with the adjectives in Activity 1.

_____

_____

Extra time? Describe your dream bedroom with the adjectives above.

1 🎧 2.04 Listen and match. Then read and write.

Lucia ☐ Max ☐ Amelie ☐

| a | b | c |

~~tidier~~   messier   the messiest   the tidiest

1 Max's room is ___tidier___ than Lucia's room.

2 Amelie's room is _____.

3 Lucia's room is _____.

larger   tinier   the tiniest   the largest

4 Amelie's desk is _____ than Lucia's desk.

5 Amelie's desk is _____.

6 Max's desk is _____.

2 Look and make sentences.

Sam's chair    **Pippa's chair**    **Bruno's chair**

1 Pippa's chair / soft / Sam's chair   _Pippa's chair is softer than Sam's chair._

2 Pippa's chair / hard / Bruno's chair _____

3 Bruno's chair / soft _____

4 Sam's chair / hard _____

I can shine! ✳

3 Draw a bedroom and compare in a group of three. Write sentences using the adjectives on this page.

Henri's bedroom is larger than my bedroom. Lara's bedroom is the largest.

_____

_____

Extra time? When you learn a new adjective, learn the opposite, too: *short – long*.

1 **Read and match.**

1 This was the first place Kim and Leo visited on the rollercoaster. Their city looked very old! ☐

2 This was the second place that Kim and Leo visited. They saw their old city square. It was more beautiful than it is today. ☐

3 This was the third place that Kim and Leo visited. This is what their city is going to look like in the future. ☐

2 **Look at Activity 1 and circle.**

1 Kim and Leo visited an eco-friendly **skyscraper / library / theme park** and went on a green rollercoaster ride.

2 First, Kim and Leo saw an ancient **castle / skyscraper / mansion**.

3 Then they saw a picturesque **library / tower / city square**.

4 In the city square, they saw a wonderful **shopping centre / palace / theme park**.

5 They also saw many traditional **mansions / towers / castles** in the city square.

6 In the future city, they saw many modern **mansions / skyscrapers / libraries**.

Let's imagine!
Tell me about the story!
'Our city through time' is a(n) **biography / adventure story**.
My favourite character is _____.
My favourite place the characters visit is _____.

I can shine!

3 **Design your own rollercoaster ride that travels back in time.**

1 What times in history can you visit? _____

2 What places in your city can you see? _____

Extra time? My city in the past, my city today or my city in the future. Which is best?

1 Look and write.

 Ryan

 Paula

 Adam

1 Paula's house is _____more traditional_____ (traditional) than Ryan's house.

2 Adam's house is _____ (traditional) of all.

3 Paula's house is _____ (picturesque) than Adam's house.

4 Ryan's house is _____ (picturesque) of all.

5 Paula's house is _____ (eco-friendly) than Adam's house.

6 Ryan's house is _____ (eco-friendly) of all.

Is your house more traditional than my house?

Yes, we live in the most traditional house in the area.

Let's build!

Ask and answer to compare homes.

2 Read and write. Then listen and check.

Simon: Let's go and stay in this campsite. It's near the beach.

Mum: No, I don't want to stay there. It's
¹___too big.___ (big) I don't want to go camping with hundreds of other people.

Simon: How about this one? It's in a forest!

Mum: No, I don't like that one. It isn't
²_____ (big). There's only one bathroom in the campsite. I don't want to wait to have a shower.

Simon: I've found it! This campsite isn't too big and it isn't too small.

Mum: No. It's ³_____ (expensive). Look at the price for two nights!

Simon: I don't think you want to go camping at all.

Mum: Yes, you're right. Camping is
⁴_____ (difficult). Let's just stay at home!

I can shine!

3 Make sentences with a partner using *too* and *enough*.

This room is too dark.

Pronunciation Colour the two sounds in red and blue.

ten   den   food   tiny   foot   to   door   do

1 Read and match. Then look and write.

1 carbon dioxide   a a gas in the air that animals and people need

2 oxygen   b things that make energy from sunshine

3 solar panels   c a gas that animals and people give out when they breathe out

4 wind turbines   d things that make energy from wind

Our cars and factories produce a lot of
1_____, which is bad for the environment.

We have to protect our planet because we all need to breathe 2_____ from the air.

We should use more green energy, for example
3_____, which turn wind into electricity, or
4_____, which turn sunshine into electricity.

2 🎧 2.16 Look, listen and tick (✓).

1 Which house does Jen want to live in?

a ☐   b ☐   c ☐

2 Which eco-friendly design does Jen want on her house?

a ☐   b ☐   c ☐

3 Which building is Martin drawing?

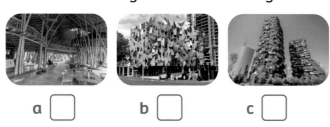

a ☐   b ☐   c ☐

Look and tick (✓) the eco-friendly things.

Extra time? What's your favourite green building in your town or city?

1 Read and answer.

Which adjectives does the writer use to describe places? _____

These three cities are amazing!

On the left is Milan in Italy. There are a lot of traditional buildings. In the middle is Sydney in Australia. There are many modern skyscrapers. On the right is Chiang Mai in Thailand. There are many ancient buildings. Milan is larger than Chiang Mai. Sydney is the largest city.

I think that Chiang Mai is the most wonderful city because it's beautiful and interesting.

 **Milan**

 **Sydney**

 **Chiang Mai**

Area: 181.8 square km
Population: about 3.1 mill. people

Area: 12,368 square km
Population: about 4.9 mill. people

Area: 40.22 square km
Population: about 200,000 people

2 Give it a go Plan your description of these three cities.

 **Tokyo, Japan**

 **San Francisco, USA**

 **Hum, Croatia**

Area: 2,194 square km
Population: about 9.27 mill. people

Area: 121.4 square km
Population: about 896,047 people

Area: 3,000 square metres
Population: 30 people

How can you introduce the three photos?	
What is in the photo on the left / in the middle / on the right?	
Compare the three cities.	
Which city do you like best? Why?	

I can shine! ✷

3 Write your description of the three cities.

_____

_____

_____

Check your work! Read your description again. Did you use interesting adjectives?

1 **Look and write.**

| full theme park   empty theme park   soft chairs |
| hard chairs   ~~modern palace~~   large tower |

1 modern palace

3 _____

5 _____

2 _____

4 _____

6 _____

2 🎧 **2.18** **Look at Activity 1 and make sentences. Then listen and check.**

1 large / tiny

a Martin's tower / Nina's tower   Martin's tower is larger than Nina's tower.

b Martin's tower _____

c Sue's tower _____

2 empty / full

a Nina's theme park / Sue's theme park _____

b Martin's theme park _____

c Sue's theme park _____

3 modern / ancient

a Martin's palace / Sue's palace _____

b Sue's palace _____

c Nina's palace _____

3 **Look at Activity 1 and say sentences using *too* and *enough*.**

Sue's theme park is too full.

Martin's theme park isn't eco-friendly enough.

18

Extra time? I'm a tall building, I touch the sky and I'm very modern. What am I?

1 Think and write. Then add an extra word to each category.

large tiny light dark tidy messy full empty ancient
modern traditional picturesque wonderful eco-friendly

I like the
inside of my home to be…

I don't like the
inside of my home to be…

2 Complete your journal.

Step 1: Imagine your dream eco-friendly home. What does it look like? How is it eco-friendly?

Step 2: Draw your house and label the eco-friendly features. Write a description of your house. Compare the different rooms.

Step 3: Finish, check and read your journal.

This is my dream home. It's a wonderful, eco-friendly mansion!

There are solar panels and a wind turbine on the roof.

My kitchen is larger than my bedroom. But my living room is the largest room in my house.

3 Think and write.

Unit 2

My favourite building: _____

My favourite new adjective: _____

Something that makes a house eco-friendly: _____
_____

Tip!
You say that you're
at home, in a room
but on a floor
of a house!

Our lives

1 🎧 (2.20) **Listen and answer.**

1 Where do Lucas's aunt and uncle live?

_____

2 Where did they go on Saturday morning?

_____

3 What did Lucas eat for lunch?

_____

4 What ride did he go on after lunch?

_____

5 How did he feel on the ride?

_____

6 How did he feel that night?

_____

2 Imagine you took a picnic to the Green Adventures yesterday. Talk about your day using the words and phrases in the box.

> went   saw   found   ate   the largest   the tiniest   the most wonderful

Yesterday, I went to an eco-friendly theme park…

3 💬 **Read, write and match. Then say with a partner.**

1 I feel very hot.
2 Maybe I should seek medical assistance.
3 I don't like this modern skyscraper.
4 I don't like this rollercoaster ride.

a It isn't traditional e_____ for me.
b So, you m_____ that you have a temperature.
c It's t_____ scary for me.
d In other w_____, should you go to the doctor?

4 Read and answer *True* or *false?*

1 Leo is going to go to Green Adventures next Thursday.   F

2 There are three areas in the theme park.   ___

3 He thought that the palace was the most picturesque area.   ___

4 He didn't want to go on the largest rollercoaster.   ___

5 He ate a sandwich for lunch.   ___

Leo, 12

I had the most wonderful day at Green Adventures last Thursday! There were three areas in the theme park with lots of rides in each area. The palace was more picturesque than the castle. But the mansion was the most picturesque area in the park. I went on the largest rollercoaster! The café was great, too. I had a delicious salad with peppers and onions.

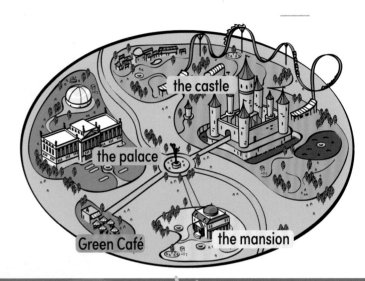

the castle

the palace

Green Café

the mansion

Mini-project

5 Imagine you went to Green Adventures yesterday. Write your review.

1 Look at the map in Activity 4 and compare the three areas of the theme park.

2 What did you eat in the café?

_____

_____

_____

_____

_____

_____

_____

Time to shine! ✳

6 Read and tick (✓).

My show programme

I can talk about healthy food.

Bravo! ☐   Good! ☐   Practising ☐

I can write about international food.

Bravo! ☐   Good! ☐   Practising ☐

I can talk about eco-friendly things and compare buildings in a city.

Bravo! ☐   Good! ☐   Practising ☐

I can write a description of a city.

Bravo! ☐   Good! ☐   Practising ☐

3 Natural world

Let's review!

Name four places in the natural world.

_____   _____

_____   _____

1 Look and write.

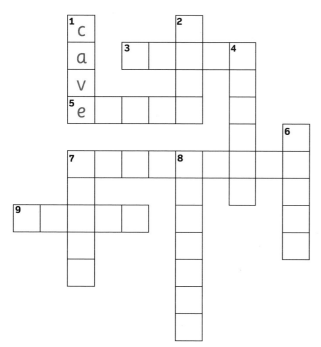

Across ➡

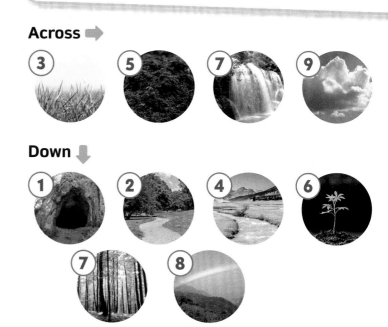

Down ⬇

2 Look at Activity 1. Then look and write.

My sister and I went for a lovely walk in the
¹ __woods__ yesterday. We walked along a stone
² _____ and saw a lot of interesting things.
We passed a huge ³ _____ and watched the
water crashing onto the rocks below. There were a lot of
grey ⁴ _____ in the sky and it started to rain.
We went inside a dark ⁵ _____ and waited
for the rain to stop. Later, we walked home and we saw
a beautiful ⁶ _____ in the sky!

Tell me!

*Imagine you went for a walk in a natural place at
the weekend. Write about what you saw.*

_____

Extra time? What natural places do you want to visit? Why?

1 (3.04) **Listen and match. Then make sentences.**

1 Lucy   **2** Tom   **3** Tessa and Rita   **4** Pedro and Nina

 **a**    **b**    **c** 1    **d**

1 Lucy _was digging the holes._

2 Tom _____ .

3 Tessa and Rita _____ .

4 Pedro and Nina _____ .

> put / earth around
> the new trees
> water / the new trees
> ~~dig / the holes~~   put /
> the trees in the holes

2 **Look and make questions and answers.**

1 a What / Sara / do yesterday afternoon / ?

What was Sara doing yesterday afternoon?

   b climb / a tree

_____

   c plant / a tree

_____

2 a What / Jan and Marie / do yesterday afternoon / ?

_____

   b have / a picnic in the woods

_____

   c have / a picnic on the beach

_____

Jan   Marie   Sara

I can shine! ✳

3 **Imagine you were on a nature trip with your family yesterday afternoon. What were you doing at three o'clock?**

We were walking along the path...

_____

_____

_____

> **Extra time?** Make flashcards with pictures to help you learn new words!

1 **Read and number.**

☐ **a** Matt and Louise get inside the Wild Weather Machine to learn about extreme weather.

☐ **b** They see a drought.

☐ **c** They design a game about extreme weather and win the competition.

1 **d** Matt and Louise find out about a competition at the science museum.

☐ **e** They see a volcano and an earthquake.

☐ **f** They see a thunderstorm and a flood.

2 **Look and write.**

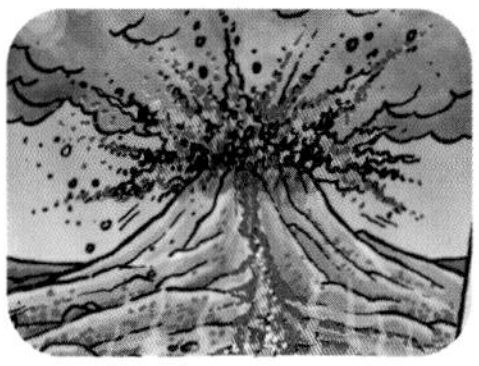

1 _____volcano_____ 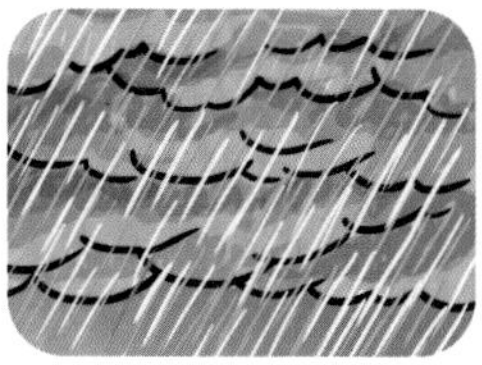   2  _____   3 _____

4  _____   5  _____   6 _____

Let's imagine!
Tell me about the story!
'The Wild Weather Machine' is a **diary / comic book** story.
The story setting is _____.
My favourite **character / part** is _____.

I can shine! ✳

3 **Imagine you were inside the Wild Weather Machine yesterday.**

1 What extreme weather did you see?

_____

2 How were you feeling?

_____

Extra time? How can you tell other people about extreme weather and climate change?

1 **Read and write.**

1 What <u>were you doing</u> (you / do) when the tornado <u>hit</u> (hit) your house?

I <u>was hiding</u> (hide) in the basement.

2 _____ (you / sleep) when the thunderstorm _____ (start)?

No, I wasn't. I _____ (have) a shower.

3 _____ (Emily / visit) her grandmother when the flood started?

Yes, she was. She _____ (sit) in her grandmother's kitchen.

4 What _____ (Petros and Louisa / do) when they

_____ (hear) the volcano?

They _____ (ride) their bikes.

Let's build!
Imagine there was a thunderstorm yesterday. Ask and answer.

2 🎧 3.12 **Read and write a–d. Then listen and check.**

What were you doing when the thunderstorm started?

I was walking to school when the thunderstorm started.

a What's it going to be like tomorrow?

b It's going to be sunny and hot.

c What's the weather like outside?

d It's sunny and cold.

Ben: Let's go to the park and play football now.

Marta: 1 _____

Ben: 2 _____

Marta: I don't like very cold weather. Maybe we can go tomorrow.

3 _____

Ben: Hang on, I'll have a look.

4 _____

Marta: I don't like very hot weather either. I'm going to stay at home.

I can shine! ☀

3 💬 **Ask and answer about the weather with a partner.**

today   tomorrow   Saturday

What's the weather like today?

It's sunny and warm.

Pronunciation Colour the two sounds in red and blue.
thi**n**   thi**ng**   everything   when   ten   swimming   raining   rain

1 **Read and match. Then look and write.**

1 hurricane
2 rainfall
3 rise (v)
4 temperature

a the amount of rain that there is in a place
b how hot or cold it is
c a storm with strong winds and rain
d to go up

A huge ¹_____ is going to hit the south of the country tonight.

It's going to bring a lot of ²_____ and strong winds.

The ³_____ is going to remain low tonight.

But it's going to ⁴_____ tomorrow, when we expect a warmer day.

2  **Listen and circle.**
(3.16)

1 What did Alex do at school today?
  a His teacher told him about climate change.
  b He listened to a talk by a woman called Anya.
  c He read a book by a woman called Anya.

2 How is Alex going to help stop climate change at home?
  a recycle more paper
  b recycle more glass
  c turn off lights

3 How is Alex going to tell other people about climate change?
  a write a blog
  b write a song
  c make a speech

> *What can you do at your school to make a difference to climate change?*

Extra time? Anya said we can all make a difference to climate change. Do you agree? Why / Why not?

1 **Read and answer.**

How do we start and finish an email? _____

Hi Sophie,

I'm writing to tell you about something terrible that happened to us when we were camping last weekend.

When I was sleeping, there was a huge earthquake.

The ground started to move and we all ran out of our tents.

We heard a loud noise and a tree fell down near the stream.

We were very scared.

In the end, the ground stopped moving and we were happy because we were all safe.

I hope that you don't have any scary camping adventures this summer!

See you soon!

Penny

2 Give it a go **Plan your email about an extreme weather event that happened when you were camping last weekend.**

Explain the topic of the email in one sentence.	_____
What extreme weather event happened?	_____
• What were you doing when it started?	_____
• What happened during the event?	_____
• How did you feel? What happened after the event?	_____
What sentence are you going to use to finish your email?	_____

I can shine!

3 **Write your email about an extreme weather event that happened when you were camping last weekend.**

_____

_____

_____

_____

_____

Check your work! Read your email again. Did you start it correctly? Did you finish it correctly?

1 **Look and write.**

Last Saturday

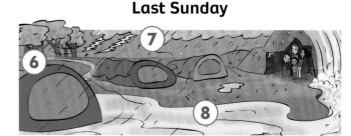

Last Sunday

1 ___path___	2 _____
5 _____	6 _____

3 _____	4 _____
7 _____	8 _____

2 **Look at Activity 1 and write. Then listen and check.** 3.20

1 What / the girl / do / last Saturday / ?

What was the girl doing last Saturday?
She was sitting on the grass.

2 What / the woman / do / last Saturday / ?

_____ ?

_____

3 What / the boy / do / last Saturday / ?

_____ ?

_____

4 What / the family / do / when / the thunderstorm / hit the campsite?

_____ ?

_____

3 **Look at Activity 1. Imagine that you were in a tent at the campsite last Saturday. Order and write questions. Then answer.**

1 the / What's / like / outside / weather / ?

_____

2 going / be / weather / to / the / tomorrow / What's / like / ?

_____

Extra time? Sometimes I'm white, sometimes I'm grey.
Sometimes I make rain, sometimes I blow away! What am I?

1 Think and write. Then add an extra word to each category.

a waterfall   droughts   clouds   floods   a rainbow
hurricanes   a cave   some rainfall   a stream

In the sky,
I can see…

Look after our natural world!

In the woods,
I can see…

Climate change means more extreme weather, for example…

2 Complete your journal.

Step 1: Imagine how you can make a difference to climate change at home and at school.

Step 2: Draw a picture of your house and your school. Write your ideas.

Step 3: Finish, check and read your journal.

I can make a difference to climate change!

I'm going to save water.

I'm going to turn out lights.

I'm going to recycle all my paper.

I'm going to ask Mr Briggs about solar panels.

I'm going to start a school environmental club.

I'm going to start riding my bike to school.

3 Think and write.

Unit 3

An amazing natural place: _____

An extreme weather event: _____

An interesting fact: _____

Something I can do to make a difference: _____

Tip!
Global warning is another way of saying climate change.

Home-school link ⬇ Tell your family about your favourite weather.

4 All about water

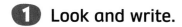
Lesson 1 ➡ Vocabulary

1 Look and write.

   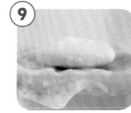 

1 _____sink_____   6 _____
2 _____   7 _____
3 _____   8 _____
4 _____   9 _____
5 _____   10 _____

Tell me!
What did you use in the bathroom this morning?

_____

2 Look at Activity 1. Then look and write.

Mum: Have you got everything you need for your camping trip?

Tom: Yes, Mum! I've got my ¹_____soap_____ to wash myself with and I've got my ²_____ to dry myself with! I've got my ³_____ to wash my hair. I've also got my toothbrush and ⁴_____ for my teeth!

Mum: Are there any ⁵_____ or baths at the campsite?

Tom: Yes, there's a bathroom in each cabin. There's a ⁶_____ outside each cabin too, so we can brush our teeth in the sunshine!

Extra time? Do you prefer to have a shower in the morning or in the evening? Why?

1 🎧 4.04 **Listen and tick (✓). Then order and write.**

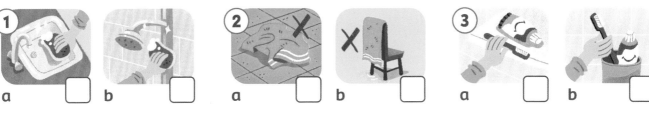

1 ①   b ☐

2 ②   b ☐

3 ③   b ☐

1 clean / We / shower. / the / must

   We must clean the shower.

2 leave / floor. / We / our / on / mustn't / towels / the

   _____

3 toothbrushes / We / must / our / put / pot. / the / in

   _____

2 **Look and make sentences.**

1 clean the sink / every morning ✓ We must clean the sink every morning.

2 use other people's towels ✗

   _____

3 turn off the taps ✓

   _____

4 have long showers ✗

   _____

5 leave soap / on the floor ✗

   _____

I can shine! ✳

3 **Write a list of rules for saving water at home.**

We mustn't have long showers.

_____

_____

_____

Extra time? Next time you're in the bathroom, point and say words in English!

1 **Read and write.**

dry   twenty-five   charity   four   five   ~~sixty~~

1 Aluna is going to be _____sixty_____ years old soon.

2 When she was young, she walked _____ kilometres to get water.

3 In summer, the stream was often _____ because of a drought.

4 Everything changed when Aluna was _____ years old.

5 They worked for _____ days to find water in the ground.

6 Aluna's daughter works for a water _____ .

2 **Order and write.**

1 We get our water from the ___water pump___ (t w e a r / u p p m).

2 _____ (a r w t e / h r c i s e i a t) dig a lot of wells around the world.

3 You can use a _____ (c t e b k u) to carry water.

4 A _____ (l e l w) is a deep hole in the ground where you can get water.

5 A lot of people around the world don't have safe _____ (l t o i e s t).

6 The water from this _____ (n i s g r p) is clean and safe to drink.

> **Let's imagine!**
> *Tell me about the story!*
> **A narrator / Aluna** tells the story 'Our journey to clean water'.
> *The story setting is*
> _____.
> *The most interesting part is when*
> _____
> _____.

I can shine! ✳

3 **Imagine that Aluna is taking you on a tour of her village. Continue the conversation.**

Hi! Welcome to my village!

_____

_____

_____

Extra time? Imagine Aluna visited your school. What questions do you want to ask her?

1 Read and circle.

1 **In the past, / In the future,** we didn't have a well in our village.

2 **Three years ago, / Now** we have a water pump in our village.

3 **When I was young, / Next year**, I had to walk to a stream to collect water.

4 **At the moment, / In the future,** there are going to be water taps in every house.

5 **These days, / Last month,** I collect water whenever I want with my bucket.

6 **Soon / Today** there are going to be safe toilets for everyone.

Let's build!
Say something true and false about your past, present and future. Can your partner guess the true sentence?

When I was young, I climbed a mountain.

Two years ago, I camped in a forest.

I think the second sentence is true!

2 (4.12) Read and write a–c. Then listen and check.

a Do you mind if I fill it up?

b Can I open the window, please?

c Could I have a drink of water, please?

Mariam:	Excuse me, Mrs Bond. I'm really hot. **1** _____
Mrs Bond:	Yes, that's fine. But I'll do it because it's very heavy.
Mariam:	Thank you! **2** _____
Mrs Bond:	Yes, no problem. Have you got your water bottle?
Mariam:	Yes, I have, but it's empty. **3** _____
Mrs Bond:	Yes, OK, but please be quick. You don't want to miss the English test!

I can shine!

3 Talk with a partner. Make requests.

① ② ③ ④

Pronunciation Colour the two sounds in red and blue.
k**i**d k**i**nd s**i**nk f**i**nd spr**i**ng m**i**ght l**i**fe v**i**llage

1 **Read and match. Then look and write.**

1 dishwasher
2 flush
3 tank
4 washing machine

a you use this to wash clothes
b you use this to clean a toilet
c you use this to wash dishes
d you use this to store water or other liquid

I do a lot of things to help save water! I always use a half [1]_____ in the toilet. I only put my [2]_____ on when it's full of dishes. I only put my [3]_____ on when it's full of clothes. I collect rainwater in a [4]_____ in my garden.

2 **Listen and write one or two words.**

Save water day!

What day?	next [1] _____Tuesday_____
Morning – Yasmin Green's talk	How can we save water [2]_____?
Afternoon	put [3]_____ in playground
Arrive at what time?	[4]_____
Wear	[5]_____ clothes
Mustn't forget	[6]_____

Say three ways you're going to save water at school.

Extra time? Why must we save water?

1 **Read and answer.**

What does Maria use to communicate her main message?

_____

Save water on holiday!

We use about 360–450 litres of water a day at home. We try to save water at home but what about when we're on holiday? We can save water on holiday, too.

Choose hotels that have rainwater tanks. Rainwater tanks collect water when it rains and use it to water plants or in toilets.

use half flushes instead of full flushes in the toilet.

Don't have baths. Take quick showers.

Water is very important. Look after it!

2 Give it a go **Plan a poster about saving water at a campsite.**

What's the main message of your poster?	
Find an interesting fact about water in the world.	
Think of three ways we can save water at a campsite.	
Draw pictures to make your ideas easier to understand.	
Add a powerful sentence to explain why we must save water.	

I can shine! ✳

3 **Make your poster about saving water at a campsite.**

Save water at the campsite!

_____

_____

_____

_____

1 Look and write.

1 _____tap_____

2 _____

3 _____

4 _____

5 _____

6 _____

7 _____

8 _____

2 (4.19) Read and write. Then listen and check.

| Now future mustn't When ~~past~~ must enough |

In the ¹_____past,_____ Aluna walked five kilometres every day to collect water from a spring. ²_____ she was twenty-five years old, her community started to dig a well. ³_____, there's a water pump in her village. In the ⁴_____, her granddaughter dreams of helping people have clean water. She wants to work for a water charity.

We ⁵_____ do everything we can to save water. We ⁶_____ waste water because it's important and there must be ⁷_____ for everyone in the world.

3 Imagine you are walking three kilometres in hot weather. Make two requests.

Could I have a hat, please?

Extra time? Whether you are dark or fair, use me to wash your hair! What am I?

1 Think and write. Then add an extra word to each category.

~~shower~~ sink full washing machine tap towel rainwater tank soap shampoo brush comb full dishwasher toothbrush toothpaste half flush

Bathroom furniture	Items you use in the bathroom	Ways of saving water at home
shower		

2 Complete your journal.

Step 1: Imagine how you can save water at home.

Step 2: Draw a picture of your bathroom and kitchen. Write your ideas.

Step 3: Finish, check and read your journal.

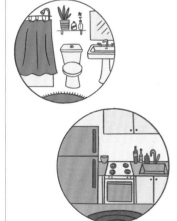

SAVE WATER AT HOME!

We mustn't have long baths. We must have quick showers.
We must use half flushes in the toilet.

We must turn off the taps.
We must only use the dishwasher when it's full.

We must have tanks in our gardens.
We must use rainwater again.

3 Think and write.

Unit 4

Most useful thing in my bathroom: _____

An interesting new word: _____

Something water charities do to help people:

_____

Something I must do to save water:

_____

Tip!
You can say take
or have a bath
or shower!

Home-school link Tell your family about how they can save water, too!

Review 2 Our world

1 🎧 (4.21) **Listen and answer. *True* or *false*?**

1 Ava and her family stayed in an eco-friendly campsite on the beach. ____

2 There was a waterfall near the campsite. ____

3 While they were putting their tent up, it started to rain. ____

4 They put their tent up next to a stream. ____

5 There were solar panels at the campsite. ____

6 There were rainwater showers at the campsite. ____

2 💬 **Imagine you were at the eco-friendly campsite with Ava. Ask and answer.**

> *What were you doing when you heard thunder?*

> I _____ .

> *What were you doing when it started raining?*

> I _____ .

> *What were you doing when it stopped raining?*

> I _____ .

> *What must we do to save water?*

> We _____ .

3 💬 **Read, write and match. Then ask and answer with a partner.**

1 What's the weather _____ outside?   a Yes, of course. I'll get a pen.

2 What's it _____ to be like tomorrow?   b It's going to be hot and sunny.

3 Do you mind _____ I borrow your tent?   c It's cold and rainy.

4 _____ I help you write the list?   d No, sorry. I need it.

4 Read and write *must* or *mustn't*.

1 I ___mustn't___ have baths very often.

2 I _____ turn the tap off when I'm brushing my teeth.

3 I _____ have long showers in the morning.

4 I _____ turn the tap off if someone leaves it on.

5 I _____ water the garden when it's sunny.

6 I _____ use half flushes in the toilet.

7 I _____ tell my friends to save water.

Remember!
I must… / I mustn't…

Mini-project

5 Make your own 'I mustn't waste water' rainbow.

I mustn't have baths very often.

Time to shine!

6 Read and tick (✓).

My show programme

I can talk about the objects in the bathroom.

Bravo! ☐ Good! ☐ Practising ☐

I can talk about an extreme weather event in the past.

Bravo! ☐ Good! ☐ Practising ☐

I can discuss and create a list of things that we must / mustn't do to save water at a campsite.

Bravo! ☐ Good! ☐ Practising ☐

I can write a list of things that I must / mustn't do to save water at home.

Bravo! ☐ Good! ☐ Practising ☐

Fair future

Lesson 1 ➡ Vocabulary

1 Look and write the words. What's the hidden job?

1

²ᶜ o o k

2 ☐☐☐☐☐☐☐☐☐☐☐☐☐

3 ☐☐☐☐☐☐☐☐

4 ☐☐☐☐☐☐☐☐☐☐☐☐☐☐

5 ☐☐☐☐☐☐☐☐☐☐

6 ☐☐☐☐

7 ☐☐☐☐☐

8 ☐☐☐☐☐☐

9 ☐☐☐☐☐☐☐☐☐☐☐

10 ☐☐☐☐☐☐☐

6 7 8 9 10

2 Look at Activity 1. Write.

1 I write stories in the newspaper. I'm a _____.

2 I look after people's teeth. I'm a _____.

3 I grow fruit and vegetables. I'm a _____.

4 I use my camera to take photos. I'm a _____.

5 I work in the kitchen of a restaurant. I'm a _____.

6 I fix cars that don't work. I'm a _____.

Tell me!
What job do you want to do? Why? _____

Extra time? Do you want to do a job where you work outside or inside? Why?

1 (5.04) **Listen and match. Then write.**

1 Henri	**2** Maria	**3** Mike	**4** Tessa
a	b	c	d

1 Henri <u>will become an engineer.</u>
2 Maria _____ .
3 Mike _____ .
4 Tessa _____ .

2 **Look and make sentences.**

1 He / get / an interesting job
<u>He will get an interesting job.</u>

2 They / not work / in the city
_____

3 I / become / a mechanic
_____

4 We / not get / bored
_____

5 You / look after / animals
_____

6 Louise / design / new things
_____

I can shine!

3 **Write about a job you want to do and a job you don't want to do.**

I'll become a mechanic *because* I love cars. I won't become a cook *because*
I don't like cooking.

_____
_____

Extra time? Learn three new words every day. Practise them with a partner.

1 Read and number.

[ ] **a** The children look at the results of a children's survey.

[ ] **b** Mrs King asks the children to write a report about their ideas.

[1] **c** Mrs King tells the children about their work for the day.

[ ] **d** The children tell Mrs King about their ideas.

[ ] **e** The children talk about what they want to do in the future.

[ ] **f** The children talk about ways to stop bullying at their school.

2 Look, read and match.

I'll do a lot of things when I ¹**grow up!** I'll ²**leave school** when I'm eighteen. Then, I'll ³**go to university** and I'll study Maths. After that I'll ⁴**get a job** as a Maths teacher. Maybe I'll ⁵**get a flat** and ⁶**have a pet**, too!

Let's imagine!

Tell me about the story!
'Children take over the school!'
is a **story / biography**.

My favourite character is

_____ *because*

_____.

I'll make a difference to bullying in my school by

_____.

I can shine!

3 Imagine that you take over your school. Write a list of things you will do to make your school more eco-friendly.

I'll put wind turbines in the playground.

_____

_____

_____

_____

Extra time? Imagine you can take over another place in your town. What will you do to make it better and why?

1 Order and write to make questions. Then answer for you.

1 university / go / Will / you / to / ?

Question: <u>Will you go to university?</u>

Answer: <u>Yes, I will.</u>

2 an / you / engineer / become / Will / ?

Question: _____

Answer: _____

3 in / Will / you / office / work / an / ?

Question: _____

Answer: _____

4 pet / Will / have / you / a / ?

Question: _____

Answer: _____

2 🎧 5.12 Read and write a–c. Then listen and check.

a We may have meetings on the computer instead!

b We could stop using planes to travel for work.

c I think we might work in eco-friendly offices.

Luke: What do you think our places of work will be like in the future?

Tina: 1 _____

Luke: Yes, and what sort of transport will we use?

Tina: 2 _____
That's bad for the environment.

Luke: But what about business meetings?

Tina: We don't have to travel.
3 _____

Luke: I think that's a really good idea!

Let's build!
What will you do when you leave school?

I can shine! ✳

3 Talk with a partner. Make predictions about the future.

1

2

3

4

Pronunciation Colour the two sounds in red and blue.
s**e**ll s**a**le plane whale then cake tell bed

1 **Read and match. Then look and write.**

1 disabled (adj)   a the same as

2 equal (adj)   b having a condition that makes it difficult for you to do some things

3 support (v)   c things you are allowed to do

4 rights (n)   d to agree with something and help it to succeed

I ¹_____ an important charity in my local community. This charity helps ²_____ people. They make sure that everyone has ³_____ job opportunities. It's important to protect the ⁴_____ of everyone in our city.

2 (5.16) **Listen and circle.**

1 Kids Take Over Day was last **Tuesday / Wednesday / Thursday**.

2 Lucy worked as a journalist on **a newspaper / the radio / TV**.

3 When she grows up, Lucy will become a journalist on **a newspaper / the radio / TV**.

4 Tom worked on his **dad's / uncle's / brother's** farm.

5 There are a lot of **cows / sheep / horses** on the farm.

6 When he grows up, Tom will become **a farmer / an engineer / a firefighter**.

7 Sam worked as mechanic at a garage near **her home / her school / the park**.

8 When she grows up, she may become a **mechanic / cook / businessperson**.

9 When she grows up, she might move to a different **area / city / country**.

> *Imagine it's Kids Take Over Day. What job do you want to take over and why?*

Extra time? Say three ways you can make your school a happier place.

1 **Read and answer.**

When we write about the future, we use _____ + _____ .

Rita

Our jobs in the future

I'm very excited about all the different jobs that my friends and I will do in the future!

I like helping people and I'm good at Science. I think I'll become a nurse and I'll work at our local hospital.

My friends will do some interesting jobs, too! My friend Paula loves Maths. I think she'll become an engineer and she'll design new things! My friend Carlo is good at taking photos. I think he'll become a photographer. He might work at our local newspaper.

My friends and I will make the world a happier place for everyone!

2 Give it a go **What jobs will you and your friends do in the future? Plan your text.**

How do you feel about getting a job in the future?	
What are you good at? / What do you like doing?	
What job will you do?	
What are your friends good at? / What do they like doing?	
What jobs will they do?	
How will you and your friends make the world a better place when you get a job?	

I can shine! ✳

3 Write your text about what jobs you and your friends will do in the future.

_____

_____

_____

_____

_____

_____

Check your work! Read your text again. Did you use *will* to talk about the future?

45

1 Look and write.

 **1** Lionel <u>will become a businessperson.</u>

 **2** Anne _____.

 **3** Fred _____.

 **4** Emily _____.

5 Luke _____.

2 🎧 5.19 Look and write. Then listen and check.

1 <u>Will Mark leave school?</u>   <u>Yes, he will.</u>

2 _____ ? _____

3 _____ ? _____.

4 _____ ? _____.

5 _____ ? _____.

3 Make two predictions about your future.   *I might become a cook.*

Extra time? When you're feeling ill, I take care of you. I help people and make them feel better, too. What am I?

1 Think and write. Then add an extra word to each category.

~~dentist~~ photographer nurse firefighter engineer cook journalist

I look after people	I create things
dentist	

2 Complete your journal.

Step 1: Imagine your dream job on Kids Take Over Day. Why do you want to do this job?

Step 2: Draw a picture of you at your dream job. What will you do? What changes will you make? Write your journal.

Step 3: Finish, check and read your journal.

MY DREAM JOB ON KIDS TAKE OVER DAY
I'll become a photographer because I love taking photos.
I'll take photos of eco-friendly buildings.
I'll make the world a better place by sharing the message with everyone about solar panels and wind turbines.

3 Think and write.

Unit 5

My dream job: _____

An interesting life event: _____

Something I will do in the future: _____

Something I might do in the future: _____

Something I can do to make the world a happier place:

_____

Tip!
You can ask, 'What do you want to become when you grow up?' or 'What do you want to be when you grow up?'

Sharing the message

Let's review!

Name four ways of sharing information.

_____ _____

_____ _____

Lesson 1 ➡ Vocabulary

1 Read and complete the crossword.

Across ➡

1 the clothes an actor wears

6 a part of a film

7 controls the camera to make a film

9 the written words the actors say in a film

10 used to mark scenes when making a film

Down ⬇

2 the music in a film

3 equipment used to make a film

4 a person who plays a part in a film

5 tells actors what to do in a film

8 the things actors use in a film

2 Look at Activity 1. Then write.

1 I love listening to the ____soundtrack____ of films.

2 I think a good _____ is really important because he or she needs to tell everyone what the film is about and why they make it.

3 A really good first _____ is important. Then I'll watch the film to the end!

4 For me, the _____ is important because that's the story of a film.

5 The _____ is important because he or she decides how the film looks on screen.

6 I really like looking at the _____ that the actors wear.

Tell me!
What makes a good film? Why?

_____

Extra time? What do you want to make a film about? Why?

1 🎧 (6.04) Listen and tick (✓) the things Josh has already done. Then order and write.

1 script. / already / written / We've / the   <u>We've already written the script.</u>

2 chosen / We've / director. / already / the _____

3 chosen / yet. / the / We / actors / haven't _____

4 the / We've / props. / already / made _____

5 camera / haven't / We / yet. / a / borrowed _____

6 yet. / We / the / haven't / clapperboard / used _____

2 Look and make sentences.

1 a Sara / already / write / the script   <u>Sara has already written the script.</u>

   b She / not write / the ending / yet _____

2 a I / already / practise / my scenes _____

   b I / not finish / my costume / yet _____

3 a Tony and Sam / already / write / the soundtrack _____

   _____

   b They / not record / the soundtrack / yet _____

I can shine!

3 Imagine you're making a film about your town. What have you already done? What haven't you done yet?

We've already chosen the director for our film – she's really good!

_____

_____

Extra time? Write words that you've already learned in one colour and words you haven't learned yet in another colour!

1 **Read and answer. *True* or *false*? Correct the false sentences.**

1 The police asked Claudette a lot of questions and then they sent her home.

[F] The police arrested Claudette and they took her to jail.

2 Timoci gave a speech at a conference in his local town in Fiji.

[ ] _____

3 Braille could see when he was a baby.

[ ] _____

4 Nickar is passionate about education for young people.

[ ] _____

2 **Look and match.**

a | b | c | d | e | f

1 write a blog   2 give a speech   3 appear on television

4 publish a book   5 make a documentary   6 share a message online

> **Let's imagine!**
> *Tell me about the stories!*
> *The stories are **folk tales** / **biographies**.*
> I'll make a difference like _____ by _____ .
> I'll share my message by _____ .

I can shine!

3 **Imagine that you're giving a speech about one of the important messages in the stories. Write notes and give speeches in groups.**

All children have the right to an education because...

_____

_____

Extra time? Imagine your teacher asks you to share an important message. What are you going to do?

1 Read and write questions. Then answer for you.

1 (you / ever / give) a speech?

Question: _Have you ever given a speech?_

Answer: _Yes, I have._

2 (you / ever / make) a documentary?

Question: _____

Answer: _____

3 (you / ever / write) a blog?

Question: _____

Answer: _____

4 (you / ever / appear) on television?

Question: _____

Answer: _____

2 🎧 **6.12** Read and write a–d. Then listen and check.

a Next, **b** In the end, **c** It's about **d** First,

Emily: Have you seen that new documentary *We All Have Rights* yet?

Mark: No, I haven't. What's it about?

Emily: **1** _____ a boy who is fighting for equal rights for old people like his grandfather.

Mark: It sounds good! Tell me about it.

Emily: **2** _____ the boy gives a speech about his grandfather's life at his school. One of his teachers has got a friend who works for a TV station so then he appears on television. **3** _____ a lot of people all over the world share his message online. **4** _____ he publishes a book about the rights of old people.

Mark: I want to see the film!

> **Let's build!**
> *Look at Activity 1.*
> *Ask and answer.*

I can shine! ✈

3 Talk with a partner about a story you've read, watched or listened to recently.

> *It's about...*

Pronunciation Colour the two sounds in red and blue.
safe save leaf leave vote value fight film

1 **Read and match. Then look and write.**

1 inspiring
2 responsible
3 successful
4 unsuccessful

a doing or getting what you wanted
b making someone feel enthusiastic about something
c not doing or getting what you wanted
d able to choose between right and wrong

My friend Zak is very ¹_____ because he works for an environmental charity. He encourages people to be ²_____ about how much electricity and water they use.

At first, he tried to share his message online but he was ³_____ because he didn't know much about the internet. But then he went on an internet course and now he's started writing a very ⁴_____ blog, which a lot of people read every week!

2 🎧 6.16 **What has each child done to share the message about Environment Week? Listen and match.**

1 Louise
2 Mark
3 Chris
4 Tom
5 Dana

a make a documentary
b write a blog
c write an article for the school magazine
d appear on school radio
e give a speech

Imagine it's Environment Week at your school. How are you going to share the message?

Extra time? What sort of film would you make to share the message about Environment Week?

1 **Read and answer.**

What does a biography say about a person at the end?

_____

David Attenborough was born on 8 May 1926 in England. When he was a child, he always loved nature. He collected bird eggs when he was seven years old!

After David left school, he went to university and studied Natural Sciences. Then, he got a job at the BBC and he appeared on television for the first time. Since then, he has made many successful television programmes about nature. He has also published many inspiring books.

David has made the world a better place because he cares a lot about climate change. He has worked hard to share this message with millions of people around the world.

2 Give it a go **Plan a biography about someone who inspired you.**

Who are you going to write about?	
When and where was he / she born?	
What did they do when they were young?	
What happened when he / she left school?	
What does he / she do now?	
Are they sharing the message about their work?	
Why has this person inspired you?	

I can shine!

3 **Write your biography about someone who inspired you.**

_____

_____

_____

_____

Check your work! Read your biography again.
Have you written about the person's life in the correct order?

1 Read and write *a, e, i, o* or *u*. Then write.

YESTERDAY

1 choose the d i r e c t o r

2 borrow a c__m__r__

3 write the scr__pt

1 ___I've already chosen the director.___

2 _____

3 _____

TOMORROW

4 choose the __ct__rs

5 finish the pr__ps

6 make the c__st__m__s

4 ___I haven't chosen the actors yet.___

5 _____

6 _____

2 🎧 6.19 Look and write. Then listen and check.

1 ___Has Laura ever given a speech?___   ___No, she hasn't.___

2 _____ ? _____.

3 _____ ? _____.

4 _____ ? _____.

5 _____ ? _____.

3 Tell your partner about your favourite film.   *It's about...*

Extra time? Put this on and become someone new, an actor wears this, how about you? What is it?

1 Think and write. Then add an extra word to each category.

~~director~~ props actor costume script camera operator camera soundtrack

People who work on a film	Things we use when we make a film
director	

2 Complete your journal.

Step 1: Imagine that you are a grown-up. What good things have you already done / haven't you done yet to make the world a better place? How are you going to share the message about the things you want to do?

Step 2: Write about your life.

Step 3: Finish, check and read your journal.

MY LIFE

I've already done a lot of brilliant things to make the world a better place! I work for a charity that fights for the right to education for everyone. I've published a book about schools and I've given a speech at the United Nations!

I also want to do something to help the environment. I haven't shared the message about this subject yet. But I want to make a documentary about the environment next year.

In the future, I want us all to work together to make the world a better place. Let's share the message!

3 Think and write.

Unit 6

An interesting job on a film: _____

Something I've already done today: _____

Something I haven't done yet today: _____

An inspiring person: _____

The best way to share an important message: _____

Tip!
You can give
a speech or
make a speech!

Home-school link 🔊 Tell your family about how they can share the message about making the world a better place.

Review 3 Our future

1 🎧 (6.21) **Listen and circle.**

1 Zak ____

  a has already filmed some scenes for his documentary.

  b has already filmed all the scenes for his documentary.

  c hasn't filmed any scenes for his documentary yet.

2 Zak ____

  a has already chosen songs for the soundtrack.

  b has already written music for the soundtrack.

  c hasn't chosen songs for the soundtrack yet.

3 Josh will become a ____ when he grows up.

  a cook   **b** mechanic   **c** businessperson

4 Helen ____ become a businessperson.

  a will   **b** won't   **c** might

5 Helen ____ get a flat.

  a will   **b** won't   **c** might

6 Zak will become a(n) ____ when he grows up.

  a actor   **b** camera operator   **c** director

2 💬 **Zak wants you to be in his documentary. Ask and answer.**

> *What job will you do in the future?*

> *Will you get a flat?*

> *Will you go to university?*

> *Will you have a pet?*

3 💬 **Read, write and match. Then say with a partner.**

1 This documentary m_____ be the start of great things.

2 What w_____ films be like in the future?

3 F_____, I talked to Josh.

4 N_____, I borrowed a camera.

a We could see more films about making the world a better place.

b Then, I talked to Helen.

c Finally, I filmed the first scene.

d I hope so!

4 Read and answer.

1 What was the first part of the film about?

_____

2 Which of Zak's friends haven't decided which jobs they want to do yet?

_____

3 What was the second part of the film about?

_____

4 Where do Zak's friends think we might live in the future?

_____

5 What do Zak's friends think we may stop doing in the future?

_____

A review: *My Friends in the Future*

☆ ☆ ☆ ☆ ☆

Yesterday, I watched Zak's documentary. It was really interesting! The first part of the film was about what his friends will do when they grow up. Josh and Helen have already decided which jobs they want to do. But Peter and Nina haven't decided yet. First, they'll go to university and then they'll think about it.

The second part of the film is about what his friends think life will be like in the future. They think that the world will be a better place! We might live in eco-friendly cities and we may stop driving cars. It sounds like a great future!

Mini-project

5 Imagine you made a documentary 'My Friends in the Future'. Write your review.

What will your friends do when they grow up?

What do they think that life will be like in the future?

_____

_____

_____

_____

_____

_____

Time to shine!

6 Read and tick (✓).

My show programme

I can talk about a documentary.

Bravo! ☐ Good! ☐ Practising ☐

I can talk about what I'll do in the future.

Bravo! ☐ Good! ☐ Practising ☐

I can understand a review about a documentary.

Bravo! ☐ Good! ☐ Practising ☐

I can write a review about a documentary.

Bravo! ☐ Good! ☐ Practising ☐

 **Goodbye** from the summer camp!

1 **Look and write.**

> toothbrush   script   waterfall   ~~pepper~~   onion   toothpaste
> tidy   rainbow   journalist   messy   clapperboard   photographer

1 _pepper_
2 _____
3 _____
4 _____
5 _____
6 _____
7 _____
8 _____
9 _____
10 _____
11 _____
12 _____

2 (7.04) **Read and circle. Then listen and check.**

1 The children **make / made** the vegetable kebabs in the camp kitchen. Mateo **ate / was eating** all the peppers.

2 Mateo's bed was **messier / the messiest** than Omer's bed. But Julia's bed was **messier / the messiest** bed.

3 While the children **was / were** walking in the woods, they saw a waterfall. Mateo **was / were** taking this photo when he fell in the stream.

4 We **must / mustn't** put the toothbrushes and toothpaste back in the pot. We **must / mustn't** waste water.

5 When Mateo grows up, **he'll / he won't** be a journalist or a photographer. **He'll / He won't** become a camera operator.

6 Su **has / hasn't** already learnt her lines but she **has / hasn't** put on her costume yet.

3 **Order and write to make questions.**

1 eat / breakfast / What / you / did / for / ?   <u>What did you eat for breakfast?</u>

2 largest / house / What's / your / the / in / room / ?

_____

3 were / What / afternoon / doing / you / yesterday / ?

_____

4 Read and answer.

Add a comment

Yesterday, I went to an amazing show at the Rise and Shine summer camp! First, we went to the camp kitchen. The children made delicious fruit and vegetable kebabs. I ate a kebab with kiwi and watermelon and my mum had a kebab with onions and peppers.

Then we visited the art area. We saw a beautiful model of a tree and some junk models of a fish. I think that the tree was more beautiful than the fish!
After that, we watched the children's film. It was all about the camp challenges. It was brilliant! My favourite part of the film was when the children picked up all the rubbish in the park.

Finally, we watched the show on stage. We listened to a beautiful poem about being eco-friendly.
Next summer, I want to go to the camp! I want to help make the world a better place, too!

>>>>

1 Where did Louis go yesterday?

Louis went to the Make the World a Better Place show.

2 What did he eat? _____

3 Which model did he think was the most beautiful? _____

_____

4 What was his favourite part of the film? _____

5 Imagine you went to a summer camp show. Ask and answer.

1 Where was it?

2 What did you eat?

3 What was your favourite part of the show?

4 Do you want to go to a summer camp next year?

I can shine!

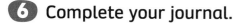

6 Complete your journal.

Step 1: Think about your favourite things in Rise and Shine 6.

Step 2: Write your journal.

Step 3: Finish and check your journal.

Goodbye to the summer camp kids!

My favourite character was Omer because he's sporty and I'm sporty, too!

My favourite thing in the show was the junk model of the fish because I like making models.

My favourite journal page was imagining what my life will be like when I'm grown up!

My favourite fact: only thirty people live in Hum, Croatia!

Home-school link Tell your family about the Rise and Shine summer camp!

Empathy Day

1 Order and write.

1 (drwrioe) _____ 2 (fsudcnoe) _____ 3 (xctdeei) _____

2 Read and write a–c. Then listen and check.

Max: 1 _____

Sophia: I feel worried. I've got to say a poem in front of the whole school today.

Max: 2 _____

Sophia: Yes, maybe! Can I practise my poem with you now?

Max: 3 _____

Sophia: Thank you so much! I already feel better!

a Yes, of course.

b **Can I help?**

c **Are you OK,** Sophia? You look worried. **Is anything wrong?**

What makes you feel worried? What makes you feel better?

World Poetry Day

3 Match.

1 li
2 poe
3 ver
4 rh
5 rhy
6 syllab

a le
b yme
c ne
d t
e thm
f se

Do you prefer funny poems to sad poems? Why?

4 Read and number. Then listen and check.

☐ **I prefer** poems about places **to** poems about things.

1 **I like** poems **more than** songs.

☐ **I like** funny poems **more than** sad poems.

Diego: ¹.... How about you?

Lucy: I don't know! I like music and poetry. But ²....

Diego: Yes, me too. When you read a poem about a place, you feel like you've been there!

Lucy: Exactly! I like poems that make me laugh, too.

Diego: So do I! ³....

Lucy: My sister doesn't agree with us. She likes poems that make her cry!

World Cities Day

5 Order and write.

1 (kieb slane) _____

2 (clpbiu ttpnosrra) _____

3 (wlrneabee gyneer) _____

6 🎧 (8.15) Read and write. Then listen and check.

> **By the way   That reminds me
> Speaking of**

Marcus: Let's go to the shopping centre.

Valerie: OK. ¹_____ shopping, we mustn't forget our shopping bags.

Marcus: Oh yes, I'll get them. OK, are you ready? I've got the keys.

Valerie: ²_____, I haven't locked the back door.

Marcus: I'll do it.

Valerie: Great. Let's go!

Marcus: OK. ³_____, you haven't picked up your handbag!

Valerie: Oh yes, thanks! I'm definitely ready now!

> *What's your favourite place in your city?*

Outdoor Classroom Day

7 Read and write a, e, i, o or u.

8 🎧 (8.20) Read and number. Then listen and check.

> Learning outside in ¹n at ur e is fun! It's ²h_____lthy because we breathe a lot of lovely ³fr__sh __ __r! ⁴S__nl__ght is good for us, too! We feel much more ⁵r__l__x__d and less ⁶str__ss__d when we're outside!

[ ] Tina: Oh, **can I borrow your** green crayon?

[ ] Matt: **Yes, of course!** Why don't we put our butterfly drawings together to make a big picture?

[ ] Matt: Oh yes, I love drawing! The butterfly is blue and red and green!

[ ] Tina: Oh yes! **Is it OK if I use your** glue stick?

[1] Tina: Look at that beautiful butterfly! Let's draw it!

[ ] Matt: **Yes, here you are.**

> *What's your favourite thing to do in an outdoor classroom?*

Word connections

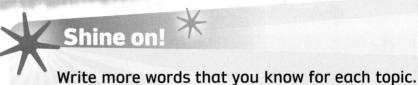

Shine on!

Write more words that you know for each topic.

Things

Welcome

door	picnic table	rope swing	window
gate	roof	seat	

Unit 4

brush	soap
comb	tap
shampoo	toothbrush
shower	toothpaste
sink	towel

bucket
toilet
water pump

Unit 6

camera	scene
clapperboard	script
costume	soundtrack
props	

Shine on!

_____
_____
_____
_____
_____
_____
_____
_____
_____
_____
_____

Food

Unit 1

chocolate	peas
kiwi	pepper
lemon	salt
onion	sweets
pear	watermelon

Shine on!

_____
_____
_____

Describing

Unit 2

dark	light
empty	messy
full	soft
hard	tidy
large	tiny
ancient	picturesque
eco-friendly	traditional
modern	wonderful

Shine on!

_____
_____
_____
_____
_____
_____

Places and nature

Welcome

cabin	summer camp

Unit 2

castle	skyscraper
mansion	theme park
palace	tower

Unit 3

cave	plant
cloud	rainbow
earth	stream
grass	waterfall
path	woods
drought	thunderstorm
earthquake	tornado
flood	volcano

Unit 4

spring	well
water charity	

Shine on!

_____
_____
_____
_____
_____
_____
_____
_____
_____

Activities and actions

Welcome

act in a film

design a programme

perform on stage

play in a band

put on a show

write a song

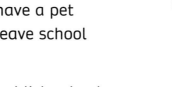
Shine on!

Unit 1

feel sick

go to the doctor

have a cough

have a headache

have a temperature

take medicine

Unit 5

get a flat

get a job

go to university

grow up

have a pet

leave school

Unit 6

appear on television

give a speech

make a documentary

publish a book

share a message online

write a blog

People

Welcome

camp leader

Shine on!

Unit 5

businessperson

cook

dentist

engineer

farmer

firefighter

journalist

mechanic

nurse

photographer

Unit 6

actor

camera operator

director